A HOT JANUARY

A HOT JANUARY

Poems 1996–1999

ROBIN MORGAN

W. W. Norton & Company   New York • London

Excerpt from "Creation" (Part 2, excerpt) translated by Judith Hemschemeyer, from *The Complete Poems of Anna Akhmatova, Expanded Edition*. Copyright © 1989, 1992, 1997 by Judith Hemschemeyer. Reprinted with the permission of Zephyr Press.

For information about permission to reproduce selections from this book, write to Permissions, W. W. Norton & Company, Inc., 500 Fifth Avenue, New York, NY 10110

The text of this book is composed in Fairfield Light with the display set in Onyx
Desktop composition by JoAnn Schambier
Manufacturing by Courier Companies, Inc.
Book design by Chris Welch

Library of Congress Cataloging-in Publication Data
Morgan, Robin.
  A hot January : poems 1996–1999 / by Robin Morgan.
    p.   cm.
  ISBN 0-393-04801-2
  I. Title.
  PS3563.087148H68   1999
  811'.54—dc21   99-25137
                                                                              CIP

W. W. Norton & Company, Inc., 500 Fifth Avenue, New York, N.Y. 10110
www.wwnorton.com

W. W. Norton & Company Ltd., 10 Coptic Street, London WC1A 1PU

1 2 3 4 5 6 7 8 9 0

Leonato: You will never run mad, niece.

Beatrice: No, not till a hot January.

—*Much Ado About Nothing,* Act I, Scene 1

ACKNOWLEDGMENTS

"Add-Water Instant Blues" and "Count Down" first appeared in *Poetry*, and were originally copyrighted, respectively, 1998 and 1999 by The Modern Poetry Association. "The Spirit Cellar" was published in the debut issue of *Poetry International*, "Tree Sister" in *Wind*, "Fixed Canon" in *Calyx*, "Referred Pain" in *The Massachusetts Review*, and "Invocation" in *Shenandoah*. "Learning Clock Patience," "Acrobats and Clowns," and "Useless Knowledge" appeared in *Ms.* magazine. *Sojourner* first published "The Butcher's Daughter," "The Farmer's Wife," "Fair Game," "The Last Time," and "Country Matters." An earlier version of "Country Matters," titled "Letter to Katherine Mansfield," was printed in *Landfall* (New Zealand). "Universal Donor" and "Samizdat" first appeared in *The Women's Review of Books*.

CONTENTS

FOREWORD

Isn't this what you knew would happen?
Sooner or later, I'd return,
the faithless lover
who thought she could escape you?
You think, therefore I am.

As if you haven't always known me
best, the one from whom I can hide
nothing, the one who knows why
poetry lives so close to madness: it is
sanity naked—the healing force,
sting, itch, scab, scar, the vital sign.

Possess me then
as no one else has, could, or ever can.
Spread me to feel my pulse insist
I Am I Am iambic at your touch.
Mark me to keep your place. Permit
your fingertips to scan my brain's
braille and sift the silk ash
pyre of these burnt images.
Believe you close and put me away
on the shelf when you are done.
| | | | |

In a Chinese ring poem,
one can start reading at any character.
In any poem,
a single character can change the world.
Rapture to rupture, for example.
Grief to brief. Morning to mourning.

Seducer, lover, ultimate intimate:
I think, therefore you are: Reader:
I am under your eyes,
I am on your mind,
I am in your hands.

PART I

LOOKING BACKWARD

Isn't this what she feared: herself-
fulfilling prophecy: a poet
might try to make sense of it?

> One definition of projection: fear's shadow
> casting its conceit across a poem's sunstruck lines.

And all the while me dreading her threat:
that I, who drafted love across her body, must
someday settle for revising it as subject matter.

> One definition of desire: the flesh made word.

The personal, political, poetic. If only they were rhetoric.
If only I could have fixed a border between them as she did,
she'd have been safe. I'd have been someone else.

> One definition of poetry:
> *imaginary gardens with real toads in them.*

Still, poets who are women comprehend being useful more
than using. If, being poets, we cherish language as we do our lives,
being women, we cherish lovers better than ourselves.

| | | | |

Poetry means refusing the choice to kill or die

The Jaguar people of the Amazon
slaughter their enemies
and use the skulls as musical instruments;

I confess to the temptation. Yet, refusing
slaughter, I play my own skull only.
But that is mine to play.

The blood jet is poetry .

A poet cannot ever understand that someone else
will never understand the act of poetry committed
not in vengeance, but simply to survive.

Poetry . . . is the skeleton architecture of our lives.

What was to me a daily passion renewing itself
warm as fresh bread, she shrugged away so often
that now she will not recognize authentic

understatement, such as: "I write these poems
reluctantly, my dear, to spare you
something worse: my death at your hands."

Suicide is, after all, the opposite of the poem.

"Therefore, lover-no-more, you are hereby unfleshed, absolved
of your reality, lust, cowardice, lies, of giving or receiving love,
of censoring yourself and words of mine that loved you. This is not

about you." This is about what got left behind.
A family. A landscape—black sand, white water, green stone.
Certain animals answering to names I'd given them.

A particular pair of boots. A claret ash tree . . .
Then, more gradually, the loss of other things.
Pride. Sleep. Health. Weight. Hair. Bone. Time. Heart. Voice.

   I must make use of myself as a found object.

The poem understands that a lover was merely the first sign,
second string, last straw. Besides, the poem knows she needs
such reassurances to believe her privacy safe from insight.

   Poetry is the moment of proof.

      The poem understands.

[Italicized lines, respectively, by Marianne Moore, Anne Sexton, Sylvia
Plath, Audre Lorde, Adrienne Rich, Diane Glancy, and Muriel Rukeyser.]

LEARNING CLOCK PATIENCE

No less and no more of merely
a card game than solitaire is: a means
of passing time in circles, as if
this radiance of unaccompanied suites
were evitable or sturdy as any other
house of cards, numbers ascending or
descending in assent or dissent, irony
at play in alternate red and black,
the colors of anarchy. "Of course,"
you say, and grin.

But such a sorting out of sorts exposes
categories we categorically reject:
kings, as always, bond;
aces, as usual, are hidden.
Still, the jacks seem tame. And here,
for once, queen seeks out queen.
Odd, in this unlikely setting,
where two grown women play at patience
sitting in a rain-enclosed verandah
on the tropical island where they came for sun.

A morning respite from wet weather
finds us exploring the interior
to meet ourselves in other skins gathered
at a stream—many of you and me,
some wearing babies or bruises, all of us slapping
laundry at the rocks, telling familiar
stories in a different language.
Our children are too thin.
Here, then, as in most places, diamonds
have more value than do hearts.

That evening, I wander through the open-air
tourist lounge and overhear a meeting;
the European men who own the island voice
mutual alarm: restless native men, it seems,
are wielding clubs and spades. Interests
must be protected, development must proceed,
a private army be imported wearing
submachine guns, walkie-talkies, smiles—Tourist
Police, they'll name it. Cigar-smoke laughter. Then
they notice me. I shuffle. And begin the game again.

Since I am white and female, they believe me
harmless. They nod and let me pass.
Later, as women do in darkness, you and I
whisper and weep about it: the coral reef

blasted to sand for trinkets, the foundation
of the first high-rise hotel, men defending
men's traditions against men imposing men's progress
while women labor for both in an interior
outside of either, telling stories
to feed their children who are too thin.

You are feverish, I am chilled.
A typhoon is expected: we cannot leave.
No one can force the cards, hurry the clock.
Each must simply play with all the skill she
can remember, learn, dare, and invent.
There's love in that, though,
and in two foolish women spending more
than they have on trinkets to feed children,
helpless to return the coral to its sea-bed anyway,
outwaiting kings and jacks gone wild,

passing the stories along to other women.
You warm my hands as I bathe your hot skull.
We try to sleep. How long, how long past midnight, then,
before wind rising slaps trees against the roof,
before the first sharp rounds of thunder are exchanged,
before I reach across a sudden flare that scours these walls
to touch the lightning shadow of your nakedness—as if
whose woman's face, rain-polished, glimmered
awake to stare in through our window, finger to lips in warning,
before the house of cards blows down?

FIREWORKS

Bright, brief, and dangerous as memory:

She'd warned it could explode in my face
and blind me, shrieked it could go off
while I was holding it and leave me marked for life.
She had a repertoire of menace: how playing in the surf
could suck me under just like that, how Doberman pinschers
could rip my throat right out, how such-and-such disaster
had killed, maimed, or disfigured so-and-so. A virtuoso
of catastrophe, she'd planned my childhood as a work to last.

But now we see through a glass lightly, decades later,
grown lovers who refuse to learn they cannot
cauterize in one another that source-wound beyond reach,
fill the lack of what had never been permitted. Your gift
was my surprise: a giant-size assortment of fireworks
that legally could be bought one day only in the year.

Yes, I was afraid.
Afraid that I'd get burned, that you'd get burned, that
sparks would drench the roof so that the house
and the whole farm would burn,
barn, sheds, gates, fences, pastures, calm-eyed

goats and cattle, all consumed in one orange roar.
I even worried the package could somehow smoulder
into spontaneous combustion
so, surreptitiously (dreading your laughter)
tried to sneak it out to the garage. Fortunate error:
I happened to glance at its list of contents in passing.

The names! Such a shimmer of names!
Devised by what great unself-
conscious bard in a Hong Kong fireworks factory?
Might such names coax me, even me, out from my fear?

> Starburst, Crackling Candle, Ruby Fire,
> Butterfly Glimmer, Fountain of
> Plumflowers, Flashing Rain . . .

What kind of wordstruck animal
wears my skin, loves sounds or marks
on a page encoding an image
as much or more than its reality?
Surely not one so innocent as to believe
poetry safer than what it describes.

> Wild Geese, Silver Chrysanthemums,
> Peacock-Feather Fan, Flying Lamps,
> Blizzard of Emeralds, Scarlet Birdwing . . .

You waited eagerly, I anxiously,

for a night unclouded, moonless,
then for dusk, then for the wind to die down.
You arranged me on the front verandah steps,
then vanished through night's curtain, emerging
match-flare cupped in one glowing, disembodied hand
below a mask that brooded eyesocket shadow, cheekbone
glaze floating where your face had been.
Then high against that jeweler's display-velour
of sky you launched your first long hissing thread of light
     to streak, burst, arc, plume
         crimson, violet, amber dazzle
            sighing down to darkness.

     Storm in Heaven. Lotus Crown.
     Fire-Opal Moon. Skywheel. Pearl Meteors.
     Golden Hive. Flametree.
     And one called simply Friendship,
     and one called simply Happiness.
     And one called Passionblaze.

Hours, hurling radiance at heaven
to dart, spin, crack its shining tail, bloom
peonies, fork lightning, spill waterfalls
in cascades of glitter. Sometimes the gesture
would go unrewarded: a bead of flame sputter
for an instant, plunge, ember, and wink out.
More often, though, what was flung upward
as an act of faith gleamed in response—

a fountain brimming azure-splashed vermillion showers,
lemon-red mandalas unfurling roses to spiral
dew down flakes of fire the color breath might be,
held in lungs of sunbleached linen.

And each release of energy flashed the garden visible,
revealing an earthbound wonder: gold-eyed animals,
a horned, hoofed, ancient audience
serenely gathered at the fence-line
waiting, like us, for the next eruption
to rinse their sight with archipelagos of luminosity.

Finally, when all the winddrift splendor
had been spent, you handed me two sticks and lit them
into sparklers so I could twirl small twin suns
in nova at arms' length, one in each hand,
too busy being God to be afraid.

The audience wandered off, then.
After such thunderclaps of incandescence
the night seemed quieter than usual. Chilled,
we went indoors. Much later, after you were asleep,
I rose and, trailing shawls, sat again on the verandah steps,
watching stars brilliant with their dying, watching
      light travel the way memory and metaphor does—
        source forgotten past naming or wonder or tears,
knowing it's not what we see but what we miss
seeing that blinds us; not what we fear but what we risk

holding of friendship, happiness, passionblaze,
that leaves us marked for life,
knowing that every moment each of us already is burning
unconsumed, and knowing, too, how rare
even the briefest visitation of pure glory is,
before it abandons us to our familiar darkness,
where we recognize the smell of sulphur in the air.

COUNTRY MATTERS

In memoriam Katherine Mansfield

Coming this late to everything
you left behind—
clematis, *kouri*, clarity's shadow
laid cool on a flush of apricot light,
flutter of hands in welcome, flutter of *tui* song,
lambs and young kids silver-lipped crying out
to suck green-swollen hills—sister
and stranger, only such passionflower words
on a page can unite us, only the silence we break
from and rave at, only the exile we're born to
which I meet again now, coming this late
to everything you left behind.

Unable to breathe colonial airs inside sharp-starched
pinafores, see from beneath wide-brimmed sailor
straws, wanting your hair wild as the *toe-toe* lewd
in the wind—was the only path out deeper down,
lit toward the nightglare of alien cities?
Was it too raw a bliss: that arch of *mamaku* uncurling
black tree-ferns, these steaming lakes and waterfalls, this sea
lit shimmering from below, that desert in redhaired-heather
lust, this film of rain a fragrance on the skin,
these terraced ochre stones scarped
in fantastic steps leading to no landing?

Or was it silence? Lies, fear, sidelong glances?
Well, you fled that cramped world—but gazing
backward as you ran, words at the bay until
they choked you, until in a distant country your blood
would feather penstrokes spelling scarlet *pohutakawa*
stamens, staining your pillow with a death.
But if you could have risked, risked anything
aloud, pealed the purest health as synonym
wrung pollen from gold *kowhai* bells—who
would have listened back at home?

Another might have heard, who wrote *"As a woman,*
I have no country. As a woman, my country
is the world." But she was plain. And older.
She heard voices. She stayed where she was—
and died of that as neatly as you died of running.
Or if you could have listened to the Maori Queen
as she sang stories in another tongue. If there had been
a place to stand, a language unbetrayed, a gesture
recognized—perhaps the words you raged unwritable,

"words without sediment," would have clung,
fine sand, volcanic, to your page. You died of it.
Their facile diagnoses to the contrary, my dear,
 you suffocated from such silence.
Sister and stranger, that lack and longing
tracks me yet: we write of country matters
yet have no place to stand, nowhere
to come this late to, having left ourselves behind,

unable to breathe in exile or at home, still
babbling bright fevers for which no remedy exists,
still gasping *"The little lamp—I seen it,"* still
as we die of it burning approximate words, not
knowing whether the gift is cure or disease
as it consumes us, knowing only the truth we cannot
find names for and, at the end, only this yearning,

as that final sigh whistles through us
and the linen is slowly drawn up
over our unblinking stare—
a drift of white, cool as a low-lying cloud:
"I seen it."
You died of it, my dear.

[The *tui* is a bird native to New Zealand/Aotearoa; *kouri, toe-toe, mamaku,*
pohutakawa, and *kowhai* are native flora. The first quote is from Virginia
Woolf, other images and quotes are from Mansfield.]

THE COOL WEB

(in respectful dissent with Robert Graves)

Children are loud to wail how real the nightmare
how mute with menace shadows glide the floor,
brazen to call on spirits, faeries, angels
unsummoned by adults who scorn such spells.

Adults have silence to delude our bedtime hell,
and silence to muzzle our menial noon.
We censor shrieks uncivil in shrill pain.
We strangle melody we dare not sing.

There's a cool web of silence winds us in,
retreat from too much fear or too much joy.
We moderate our meanings to appease:
articulating silence through our lies.

But if we broke the truth, the troth, the chains
and gags, the hush, then we would break a dawn
dispelling ghosts that walked where we, undead,
might name ourselves mere mortal angels, yet still
cry praise. For only the revenant unspeakable, unsaid,
will stalk, haunt, rise in the throat, and kill.

THE FARMER'S WIFE

I'm not who you think I am
leaning against the kitchen doorframe
twisting this stained apron in scarred hands.
I was bleeding from something.
Maybe the blackberry thorns
where I went picking for jam. Maybe rescuing
that newborn kid caught in the brambles,
fleeceflakes puffed on the barbs where she'd spun
and spun to free herself, only getting trapped deeper.

I'm not who the neighbors think I am
when they come with carrotcake and I serve them tea
and they talk about the weather and sports
and the market price of wool and I smile and nod.
To them I smell of onions and bleach, and even
after a bath, of the pigsty I shoveled out and hosed
all morning, my one satisfaction: bringing order
to chaos, gleam to dullness, freshness to whatever reeks.
When I smell myself, I smell something burning.

I'm not who the farmer thinks I am, either. I used to fear
insects. Now I see them as makers of honey and silk. I'd like
to make honey or silk. I used to love someone, maybe this farmer

I watch now, out checking the stock, peering to see
if the pasture's greened up again after the rains, turning
homeward. I should set out the bottle, the matches, the smokes,
turn off the music. I don't want a fight. When I'm all by myself,
I play Bach on the stereo—the Passions, Saint Matthew, Saint John.
I hate God, though.

Only those people who never went farming think farming's
about growing things. Mostly farmers kill things. Mine,
who says little, says you just have to, and sets possum traps,
lays rabbit poison, strews rat bait, scatters slug pellets, sprinkles
insecticides, fungicides, herbicides, chloroforms, collects
loppers and mowers, weed-eaters, spray guns. My farmer is skilled
in the use of such tools and techniques. I'm not.
But I'm learning you just have to be. Maybe
I'm not who I think I am, too.

MESSAGE MACHINE

"The lie is the child of silence." —Ursula K. Le Guin
"When it comes to atoms, language can be used only as in poetry."
—Niels Bohr

Hello, I'm not here.

    A silencer makes the weapon more effective.

        What means consent, is golden, equals death?
        No comment.

        Observe a moment of, hold your, speak
        only when, don't ask don't, neither
        confirm nor, you have the right to remain.

I can't take your call right now.

    Tell me about the silent partners, the strong
    silent types, those who suffer in silence,
    those who are seen and not heard.

        Talk about unspoken rules,
        inadmissable evidence,
        unmentionable truths,
        unnameable fears.

Let's hear it
for the cruel,
perfected,
notorious
silence of god.

Leave your name, the time and date, and where you can be reached.

I am the cloud across the sun, the faint chill wind
that makes you reach for a sweater while at lunch.

It's always midnight when mimes and trappists
sound each other out.

In New Guinea, every one of the Dani people
speaks
eight languages, tells stories in which wordplay
on a single pun lasts for two hours. Indonesia is
imposing
a uniform mainland tongue. This erasure is named
"language death."

I'll get back to you when I can.

I will have left by then,
bearing a word in my mouth
like a coin, for the passage.
| | | | |

Odysseus, Kafka knew, might have escaped
from the sirens' singing,
but from their silence, never.

Poetry is the art of the impossible.

Wait for the signal before you speak.

A HOT JANUARY

Two, in fact. Two years in a row, two hemispheres,
two women (one pair, that is, of lovers), two methods in it,
two degrees of separation. Or is it more? What space/time map
located Hell in the two-faced month where I was born?
How can a woman run mad be expected to know?

One January was so far south that rough winds
do shake the autumn buds of May there: antipodes
that can, depending more on attitude than latitude,
float on the world's summit rather than down under.
(Trust true north and not true love when the wind is southerly.)

The second January northern though freakish: El Niño,
jetstreams, greenhouse-affecting a planet's anguish
in fumes of pre-spring record warmth between snowfalls.
(And does each woman kill the thing she loves?)
But that's just weather.

Climate's something altogether different.
Two separate hemispheres, years, women; a single reason.
Or (no woman is an island) was it two? How can a woman
unbalanced for lack of equatorial temperance,
a woman for all seasons, know? I know

some things, though. I know geography
is a mirage: it exists in space; that is, in time. Time also
is an old illusion. Did I say two years? Or was it ten in all?
Fifteen? Forever? Never? Well, for a while, at least,
our arrogance was all that mattered. We called it love.

Ahead, we'd say, of our time, we scoffed at distance, age, class,
culture: delusional concepts, like race. Or madness. Or woman's
inhumanity to woman. The science reporter on TV inquires,
"But what designer would make the central facts of existence
an illusion?" "Natural selection," the biologist smiles.

Still, context isn't Nothing. Back to space and time.
"But who knows where or when?" the song complains.
I don't, don't ask me. I do know (foolish fond old woman
marking anniversaries) it had been fifteen since we met,
ten since the passion reeled us, six since it ripened us

to commitment . . . what *is* commitment? Something
to a lover or to an asylum? And asylum—is that to do
with safety or with madness? There was a two,
too, somewhere. Was it that solid flesh could melt
at her touch? Was it too much silence from her

or too many words from me? Hundreds of native words
for snow in Alaska, sand in Morocco, wind in Tibet,
hundreds for love in the indigenous me—especially
the dense interior regions where, pre-first contact,
the ancient dialect had hundreds of words for fear alone.

Easy to get lost there, here, where—? Oh yes, the two hot
Januaries, when much learning made me mad. Perhaps I never
wrote nor woman ever loved. Still, I once sang (harmonious
madness) how we were two women, how women were different,
how women knew how to love. But that was in another country,

and besides, the wench I was is dead—or good as dead,
so altered by the effort. Nothing half-hearted, by god, a full-peal
attempt it was, audacious as the chimes we, transfixed, heard
the bellringer at Canterbury blister himself trying
for a full hour one English spring—look

where the willows weep back from the photo album! Such a fine
madness: so many flat embraces, two-dimensional smiles,
so many airports, customs, languages, beds, cities,
canyons, shores, deserts and mountains, geysers and glaciers . . .
If the brain has no nerve endings how does it stutter such pain?

What a piece of work is a woman!
One seeing too little in too much, the other
seeing too much in too little—that last a poet's
occupational disease, leaving me not for the first time
with only this pen to parry, this paper to trust.

Scissors cut paper, stone smashes scissors, a paperweight
heart with a blizzard inside can trump stone—is that right?
No, fire burns paper, water drowns fire, air parches water.
That's it. Then terror gulps air. But nothing calms terror
like grief. Grief helps us grow simple.

| | | | |

Simply, then: one January summer you find yourself
digging out daily from drifts of cruelties so subtle you choose
to mistrust your sanity rather than recognize lovelessness.
A year later, older and colder from more giving and forgiving,
you finally harvest truth from your beloved's crop of lies. Rue

with a difference indeed. Reality shatters then, along
with what's left of health. Your fever, rising, seems to melt,
thaw, and resolve the earth itself, whose frail shoots rush
to the coming killer frost the way hope, obsessive crocus
upgreening through your sleep, lies blasted and deformed
    each dawn.

How tedious this mourning over a lover is, how trite! Better
to dwell on my country's shift to the Right, better to fight
for houseless heads, better to heal the body, attempt full-peal
to write. Better not ask why cheap emotion costs so much,
not wait more nights through for any answers to the bitter chant

what
    was she who
        am I where
            are my kind?

Those were the words for ice that had not been imagined.
That was the place, desolate, where the silence
she lied she loved so seized me at last by the throat

and wouldn't let go
and wouldn't let go
and wouldn't let go

until I had died of it
until what died out of me

left a cut out woman
with air in the eyes,
scissorlips rusted open,
stone tongue tolling poems.

But I fear I am now in my perfect mind.

For a new question persists
What is it women in women do require?
and an old answer insists
The lineaments of gratified desire.

[Various lines throughout this poem play off or echo phrases by William
Shakespeare, Oscar Wilde, John Donne, Robert Whittinton (on Sir Thomas
More), Robert Burns, Lorenz Hart, Percy Bysshe Shelley, Christopher Marlowe,
Michael Drayton, and William Blake.]

PART II

THE BUTCHER'S DAUGHTER

Her chin was sharp as a crescent moon
faint bloodstains gloved her fingers
she'd a taste for meat and an eye for doom
and she wielded words like cleavers.

She had played in many a fleshed boudoir
and had a way with women
and she knew how to work in an abbatoir
as if that were a given.

I was not yet used to greens and grain
but already deaf from violence
so she offered a jar to soothe my brain
afloat in a brine of silence.

Only when I'd been stunned and slit apart,
hoisted, racked, and skewered,
when her scales displayed my chilling heart,
could you finally call me cured.

SMALL TALK BLUES

Holding the phone, unseeing I stare
at the wall of my bedroom, a blank painted space
where for years until yesterday morning, my dear,
a picture hung, framing your unpainted face.

Your name on my lips once made me rejoice.
Now I'm too tired for anger. Now you're lying to me,
Now someone you're not is using your voice,
and long distance is longer than it once used to be.

A book I've just read, a film you just saw,
and a respite of course to mourn the day's news.
Somewhere there's always a war to deplore,
and we're principled people who've each paid our dues.

We murmur "Stay well," "Watch yourself," and "Take care,"
then hang up the phone. The dial tone falls still.
But the prodigal lovers you and I were
are somewhere off paying the bill.

Here, static stutters that truth's not a choice
and endings aren't civil and love has no shame.
Here someone you're not is still using your voice,
and someone I was won't stop wearing my name.

THE LAST TIME

If I had known the end was finally near
—rancor rising faster than the speed of night,
no way to check its course or to outrace it—
could I have found a courage to press that act,
fresh-petaled, silky, intimate, sly, permitting
memory of what, in losing such a loss again, is doubly lost?

There were so many early warning signals
the late ones seemed redundant. If I had realized—
this will be the last time, here, now, this kiss
the final tasting, this laugh the suffocation
of fullthroated lust between us, this night the last
of grazing hungrily each other's flesh,

this sight at the departure gate the permanent
blinding, when parting lovers tell themselves
they wave at one another but actually salute
the widening space between—if I had known,
would it have made a difference
other than one intensifying pain?

Or is such ignorance the only innocence we know,
the sole true mercy: the crumb, unnoticed, fallen
from the feast of some forgetful god long lost as well,

who, even if found or resurrected, would be as blessedly indifferent to all our little dyings as we are ignorant of them, and ignorant as we are of the hour of our death?

THE PASSION

Loving the hated subject, hating the love,
living on longing and nearing the end

every held breath of intimate absence,
every night's panic praying for sightings

every day manic in tracking the prey,
learning where to stand vigil, when to pursue,

how to decipher each clue to interpret such silence,
how to invent secret signs of requital, how to stay

pure, absurd, dangerous, ready to outwait
eternity, rabid, obsessed, patient, mad

as the mystic or saint who learns stalking,
like God and like genius, is in the details.

FAIR GAME

"Why should I blame her that she filled my days with misery . . . ?
. . . what could she have done, being what she is?"
                                        —"No Second Troy," W. B. Yeats

Not to deny the pleasure we put each other through,
lips eyes wrists thighs, rib-sore laughter,
one body's arc strung taut against the other's bow,
brains singing arrows through the air.

Not to deny all we witnessed together,
much earthly loveliness, such human grief;
not to deny how I longed to wring her throat as well
as kiss it, anything to open it so she might speak.

Not to deny she persisted ignorant to the last
both of her demons and her absolute beauty.
But not to deny I denied what I knew from the first:
We were utterly doomed, and I was bitterly happy.

USELESS KNOWLEDGE

"If only you knew from what rubbish
Poetry grows, knowing no shame."
     —"Creation," Anna Akhmatova

Coffee black, tea with milk, marmalade and chocolate bitter,
red meat, garlic, beer, wine, grass. Label: "Recent Lover."
File near a husband's relish of cheese and macaroni,
one lover's lust for venison, another whose hunger ran to lobster
Cantonese at three A.M., another who baked peach pies
but ate them all, and one who was a vegan.

Why, at times lacking specifics from the day before,
must the brain's garage shelter such clutter, data etched
in synaptic granite by loss? How dare the cells still store
that favorite red-handled paring knife with the keen edge,
the piano's thudded middle D, just how far to grope in the dark
for the lamp, which positions in lust were favored by whom?

Sitting in a New York subway car, I know all four
secret places where the hens would hide their eggs,
how to find the spigot that fed water to the lower troughs,
herd goats, clip hooves, use fly-strike powder, sort
sheared fleece for baling, mix formula to bottle-feed
abandoned kids. Unasked, circuits still encode driving

the left side of the road (but massaging that right shoulder),
still remember the precise turn then tricky swerve toward

the sole nearby town with decent olive oil. Never to return now,
how do I purge that storage, shed those once-prized skills,
let it all gladly go—Atlantis lost again, sinking forever slowly
beneath the waves? Some hoard such knowledge; you can see

them stagger under it, no strength left for learning one new thing.
Some suspect all knowledge is useless, so trade it to hear birds
descant in Greek. But some commit detailed remains to a poem's
kiln, in whose white fire nouns cremate, rising aflame as verbs
to shift perspective forever before they disappear:
useful as the central vanishing point in a Vermeer.

SAMIZDAT

Glorious leader, bemedaled and embalmed,
you lie at last a relic, marble-biered in state,
while masses of my peasant selves, black-shawled,
file past to view what was my tyrant heart.

Your guards believe us mourners: poor, ignorant
but loyal serfs come to pay due respects.
How can they know we shuffle by and squint
through glass and garlands at your features' wax

only to ensure those eyes are really shut,
those gloved hands can fist no salutes at legions,
that corpse not lunge the balcony to rant,
spellbinding us with fresh exhortations:

to sacrifice, trust, starve, and—the refrain—
willingly suffer for your sake again?

ADD-WATER INSTANT BLUES

Got to get
over you, out of here,
through with this, real,
hold of me, back my soul,
by, with it, cool.

Got to get
up for it, down to it,
on with it, strong,
a grip, a life, past it,
clear, even, along.

Got to get
off of this, into it,
going, wise, done,
got to *get* it, get free of you:
Ready. Set. Gone.

THE GHOST OF A GARDEN

The world was all before me, there to lose.
You had your other gardens—kitchen, cutting, orchard—
so the oval plot beside your house would now be mine,
you said. You withheld collaboration, claimed this must
be all my doing, swore I should plant for our future, plan
how what I did would look in twenty or more years.

Grateful and in love, I vowed this garden would reflect us.
So I studied catalogs, jotted down dreams, sketched images,
devised a sensual avant-garden fierce with blues and burgundies.
Your cobalt cornflower intensity, your vermillion drowse of poppies,
already rooted there, were welcome. To this I'd add black-knight

delphinium, hyacinths deepening from indigo to sapphire,
a Spanish lavender less mauve than darkly orchid, lobelia
lush as a Russian princess in garnet fringe, cosmos (the name!)
in winey chocolate. I would propagate violas—tiny Venetians
at Carnivale, their velvet masks hand-painted claret, maroon, sable.
I ordered a Persian lilac, and planted succulents to border

on shock: roseate cactus, magenta with black-tipped spines.
Last—the lyrical risk—a few ghostsilver shadows
to glimmer through dusk: artemisia, moonflower, lilies of the valley.
| | | | |

It did not occur to me that such a garden was a living
bruise, trailing wisps of gauzy bandage.

Already there was less heart's ease between us and more rue.
So I should have seen it coming—your newest rule:
I must not move whatever you'd already planted in this garden
that you claimed was mine to do with as I wished.
I was confused. Until then, your forget-me-nots and touch-me-nots,
self-seeding contradictions, had been hard enough to uproot,

though I did manage to relocate your chorus line of coral bells.
But now, by fiat, blighted roses (bubblegum-bright pink) must stay.
And fat bush daisies, perky as sunnyside-up-fried eggs. And neon-
orange calendula, nodding in coy denial of problems you
would not discuss. Some year you might yourself transplant them,

maybe not, you were busy: "Be patient," you snapped. I was patient
    enough
to understand you never meant to be ungenerous. This was your way
of giving: partial, controlled, revocable. As if you mistook yourself
for a jealous god: "This garden is for your delight—*but!* It is
forbidden to go there, touch here, eat that, grasp this." Worse:
I was a true believer, naked and unashamed, certain it *was*

all my doing, my devotion that would—in twenty or more years?—
redeem us from your wrath. If only I had planted fewer passion-
flowers, less of my bleeding-heart, your adder's-tongue and devil's
    tears,

our domestic violets, not settled for love-in-a-mist more than
honesty, a flower you confessed you never could quite recognize.

In the end, not all my watering could stave off the drought.
So I rebelled, was cast out, took my solitary way.
Soon after, you drove yourself, too, from that garden,
citing a score of reasons other than shame: that you'd been
naked there, or fear: of watching how what despite myself
I'd seen would look in years to come—perennial.

Neither of us broods now in that drafty house, weeds
those gardens. Whoever does, no matter how ploughed over
that oval's tilth aslope the lawn, may be unsettled
at how many decades it will take to lay the ghost
of a garden, purge the dust of love-lies-bleeding.

I work my own plots season by season now, as befits an atheist.
I discriminate each subtle shade of green. I grow what feeds
and heals: grapes, sage, solomon's seal. Still, the apple sapling
blossomed this spring. And the array of poet's narcissus
I'd once bedded to gleam chaste as pearl came up naturalized:
proud stands brazening perfume, iridescent, wild.

PART III

UNIVERSAL DONOR

In memoriam James Byrd, Jr.

". . . this, like to a murd'ring piece, in many places gives me superfluous death."
—*Hamlet*, Act IV, Scene 5

She lived her whole life knowing the truth
and one day learned it.

She knew her species invents tribes and races,
knew people murder, men hunger, children are beaten,
knew women are raped, wrapped, carved alive—
and this is called love. She knew how bulbs stink
as they rot from man-made hot winters.
She knew animals suffer and die, lovers can smile and lie.
She bore witness, fought back, knew blood as a count,
bank, sport, guilt, blood as a pressure, a debt.

There was a moment of warning, when love breathed her
deeply as surf inhales shore, when she knew blood as a heat,
thirst, pulse, lust, a sugar, a letting, a tie. Then there was a wound,
not instantly fatal, but it would serve: blood as a test, a curdling
of every sweetness she'd known. Let's say a lie—a white one,
by a lover—inflicted the wound: self-righteous betrayal
is always effective, although the victim cries out
How can you stab and stab and shout Don't bleed?

Something, at any rate, made the first puncture. Everything
else leaked in through that wound. Reality's crust

peeled like a scab and she pounded her head on the floor
for what it remembered, because now she knew blood as a poisoning,
as a line, a sucker, a type. Dizzy, she felt herself start
to change shape. She turned into a grief hunched on a bed
rocking backward and forward, whispering to an empty room
I thought we were different. Then she grew feral.

She became an old cat, deaf, trailing her hind legs,
wauling from fright. She became a wild horse, eyes rolling
with dread, cornered for slaughter, an albatross slickened
by oil, a calf in a cage. Comforters clucked at such bleakness:
an unprofligate daughter suckling, they feared,
at her wounds. But she snarled *Why should I heal and not howl?*
Because now she knew blood as a vessel, a kinship,
a group, stream, root, stone.

Let's say that she lived. One day she was shocked
to hear herself laugh *Who? Oh yes, that was a lover of mine.*
Then she knew blood as a relative, blood as a bath,
as a flow. In time the wound closes
almost. But what enters remains, coursing the veins, convulsing
its host, sudden, malarial, until death do them join. One night,
for example, she hears on the news what she knows she has no
right to be. Yet now past that point, she can no longer help but
    become

a lame old man, hitching a spring night's ride home. She becomes
being beaten and she becomes chained by her ankles to a pickup
    truck,

dragged by three young white men who hate blackness, hate what she's become: blood as a stain, vengeance, curse, clot of terror. Her dentures rattle, fall out. How will she find them she panics until her left arm shreds away, then her ribcage cracks open, then she can't shriek anymore since her head wrenches off of her neck but she can think *Now* as it rolls *Now I know* to the side of the road she can

still think *What will I do now I know* into a ditch she can think *What will I do now I know blood as an oath?*

THE SPIRIT CELLAR

A cold place and dark
the spirit cellar.
You grope in vain for a switch of light, a door,
hatch, tunnel, window, or—blind fingertips practicing
scales on air—rediscovery of wine racks, or jars
wool-clad in dust, sentry on splintery pine shelves.
Raspberry jam, maybe, or long-ago homemade
black-plum preserves gone crystallized to sugar,
pickled beets, even overwintering bulbs perhaps—
any signs of sustenance
you must have once laid by
against just such a moment.

Only shadows put up to feed on? recollections
too well preserved? Only this
sleepy lack of hunger you suspect
means you are now quite near starvation? Eat
bitterness, then, lest it devour you first.
Lick moisture from the walls of memory.
But most of all, stop plotting
how you can escape, stop
disbelieving how you got here.

Save your energy. It will cost everything
you never knew you know
simply to be where you are now.

EXTREME MEASURES

"The higher you are, the safer you are, because you have more time to deal with it in case of emergency." —Sky Diving Manual
"The deeper you are, the more in danger you are, of death from depth ecstacy."
—Scuba Diving Instructor

When I am dying
take no extreme measures.

I will be safely
in danger.

I have had time
to deal with it,

this gravity
pull toward ecstacy,

this flight from mediocrity,
this lifelong emergency.

FIXED CANON

In memoriam Eve Merriam

Elephants never call suicide hot-lines, never leave notes.
One simply dies again and again, rerunning
on the nature program, eyes rapt with pain, trumpet
fear screaming, an articulate innocence ringed by ivory
poachers—not evil men: poor men from poor countries,
wanting only the good life, hot-lines, reruns. An elephant
never bathes alone, the narrator says. But not for safety's
sake. For company. These days I bathe alone,

keep selective company, keep thinking of your final poems,
months: how roguish you looked in your plum velvet beret; cheek-
bones still more elegant than gaunt; bitter, witty plans to fight
the cancer, write the wrong to your last breath. Such a death
makes suicide unthinkable and promising, more than the poet's
occupational hazard. You did not choose it. But you thought about it.
A far cry from Antigone, these days, space-cadet cultists
hitch their wagons to a comet, teen fundamentalists seek

manliness in martyrdom, eternity's a unisex cologne commercial.
These days, reliable techniques to keep on going—"I'll celebrate
those six fringed lemon tulips exuberant in that blue bowl"—
falter in hilarity or boredom. I manage by barest
curiosity: for instance, wondering what might happen if

scientists played tapes of elephant-song to whales and the reverse.
Could one life-form imagine the existence of the other
the way I strain now to recall how utterly real you were?

Your poems, notes left behind, pray to be cured "of dying to live
forever." But the elephant dies and dies again, this time trying
to escape the circus: now *there's* a climate of hilarity and boredom.
News bulletins rerun this massive grey matter who charged
the guards "Almost as if," one shrugs, "she wanted to get shot."
Such profound insights characterize my species. Meanwhile,
in California, another whale has beached itself, leaving no note.
For company?

ARCTIC STATION

They never tell you
it's not a dark night of the soul
but a season
      breath-held for months
      far north of the heart to a silence
      windless in darkness
            sucked hollow as teeth
            of all daybreak, brittle as ice
            but more clear, thicker, pitiless.

They never tell you
dread is not trembling or sickness
but stillness
      in darkness, windless
      the frozen wastes at the pole of your life
      where you crouch
            under stars themselves ice
            flecks floating due north of the soul
            long past comprehending incomprehensible cold.

Why don't they tell you
it lasts not a night but a lifetime
drab as the comfort of fools

Why do they name sole
what's plural and common: dark everydays
of all souls who dare pay attention
        Why do they speak of one night
        and not of the first, as if
        morning would cure it

as if that were the worst of what waits
        indifferent in darkness to how you fear
                suffering thaw blister through you

beneath northern lights long despaired of
        their windprism brilliance ablur only now as you drowse
                deeper down shock melting slow shock of truth.

COL TEMPO

For Isel Rivero

(after Giorgione's La Vecchia *in the Gallerie dell'Accademia, Venice)*

Bucolic landscapes had all but put me six feet
deep down under: I was in need of beauty
forged by human hands. Where better than Venice
to walk for days and watch that chiffon light
revise reality, inviting the eye
to recognize how energy lives not in structure
but in the space around it?

Shopwindows glimmered with masks, partial or full
disguises, a wardrobe of expressions for the face
of any romantic cynic winking back my own old
metaphors. I stayed one stride ahead
of my footsteps' echo until I turned a corner
to come upon a painting I had not met before:
Giorgione's *The Old Woman*, finished at age thirty

just before he died, "given over to melancholy,"
the guidebook claimed, after having "abandoned
the precise definition of his early years."
Her eyes, rheumy with unbrimmed tears from seeing
too much, studied me back. Her coarsened features
hung slack on a skull impatient to emerge
from its wispy cap of dull pewter hair.

| | | | |

Lips bitten and chapped by silence were parted to whisper
some message, exclaiming only a gape of yellow
teeth. But her hand, pointing to the heart hidden
by sagging breasts, uncurled a slip of paper
offering me the words "Col Tempo": *With Time.*
Certain moments define how one will live
from that point on—impasto on the soul.

What was yet to come danced masked in mercy
from me then: the hours of waiting, penumbral
of a former self, knives, needles, sharp,
shallow breath held in the plang and whirr
of an MRI pod, living corpse encasketed,
unstrung instrument lying attuned as if
in an avant-garde decomposition suite.

What was yet to come—the great landscape
of pain—was masterpiece, sucking each nerve,
leaf in the tempest, into its perspective's glaze:
a foreground where it still is possible to stare
calm through spasms' nausea, a middleground where fever
aches lush through live hair, a background brightened
by fear forking clouds that brood on ruins beyond

a bridge to health one can no longer cross.
With time, whatever we've dreaded was not excessive.
With time, I would be given over, stretched, and primed
into an energy unmasked, self-pitiless, living

no more in structures my early years defined.

But that day, I saw only what an artist always sees,

and wept to recognize the self I'd fled to find.

REFERRED PAIN

After sufficient suffering, flesh becomes metaphor,
learns to let go. Fanatic, the will insists, plotting
its own day after tomorrow. All along, the elegant heart
has practiced how to transcend. But the brain is alive

with rebellion. Curious, cool, it persists, records, translates,
remembers, tries, tries again: a clock of physics second hand
bent straight circumference to pivot, every- and no-
where at once (twice, squared, and also later).

Here numbers circle our faces infinite
metaphors tricked in crystal until laughter shatters us
apart and they escape: an idea of god as entropy,
self-referential, a brain warning each universe

it creates, "You must be racked, hanged, burned alive
to learn what metaphor requires from those who ride it"—
but then appeals Do this in memory of me:
Recognize yourself

as metaphor, a thought wheeling
solitary, luciferious,

in freefall through space,
still noticing:

So this is lungburst while the sky careens
above an earth jerked out beneath my weight.

So this is dying, to rise arrayed in skintight flame.

So that was the illusion of a body. Interesting.

INVOCATION

Gunmen attacked a school in northwestern Rwanda last Monday, killing seven-
teen girls. . . . The attack took place after the Hutu gunmen ordered the girls to
separate into groups of ethnic Hutu or Tutsi, and the students refused to comply.
—the New York Times, April 30, 1997

Insane, sadistic gods to whom I offer
only my denial and disgust,
how do we bear witness to each other
when such defiance gleams beyond our trust?

They stupify us, these small, nameless girls
in whose name Love linked arms with her best friend.
Courage skulks shamed before these little skulls
rotting on the grassy school playground.

Let me be worthy of such children, slain
where they stand, who in the face of dying, cling.
Let me be equal to my small, sufficient pain
and in the broken teeth of horror, sing.

CAVE DWELLERS

1. The Glowworm Caves, Waitomo, New Zealand

Every tourist enters a cave uneasily.
This one is narrow, chilled, dank—water leaching
from fissures veining the walls, the ground slippery,
springy. Skin becomes moist, or is that sweat
from fear? The air is stifling, too thick with echoes
of a distant *om* from subterranean rapids.
The only way back is ahead.

But then the tourist stumbles into a room-size galaxy,
to crane aghast at sequins of light spangling
the low-ceilinged dark, rippling bright or dim
in time to currents of air draughting the chamber.
The tourist sees spectacle, entire constellations
shimmering deep underground. The tourist blinks,
awestruck at such gratuituous splendor.

Splendor is never gratuitous,
and only the strong should risk learning
how and why beauty is forged. Each glowworm
excretes and then dangles almost seventy threads.
The eggs are laid so the larvae live in the threads

eating trapped insects drawn by the light
given off as a lure by the worm while it dies.

The tourist does not see these million
microscopic rituals of birth and murder,
a brutal loveliness indifferent
to curiosity, disgust, or praise, a splendor
gratuitous only in the sentimental gaze
of every fearful tourist drawn by the same lure
of light down into the dark.

2. *The Altamira Caves, Santillana del Mar, Spain*

How wonder must have fed her, the nine-year-old
straying from her father's foraging for arrowheads
and flints, who followed a trail of geometric figures
and handprints, then cried out "Oh look, look up, oh look up
there!" pointing through the torchlight at whole herds
flickering wild with color, movement, and dimension,
unwitnessed for more than fifteen thousand years.

Horned, bearded bison grazing, galloping, curled asleep
in black and ochre; horses standing, heads turned;
a female boar fluid in midleap, a flock of mountain
goats, small black bulls lowering, and—engraved
and scraped as well as painted in strokes
so delicate nostrils still flare beneath that wide
fringed eye—the life-size, perfect, startled deer.

No one knows who did this or how or why, who
worked by the glow of smoky peat fires, squatted
or kneeled in these corners or lay flat, cramped, face up,
to paint, as another would later do; who conceived
of using the rough protuberances of rock as natural relief—
this bulge a bison's hump, that hollow a horse's flanks; whose
eyes burned with the effort to revision precisely a running form.

Experts argue meaning: totems for the hunt, perhaps?
a sacred sanctuary? a site for magic rites? Magic indeed,
that outwits darkness, outwaits time; magic
that drives some prehistoric child to press a handprint
in the damp clay wall another child will find; magic
that compels some Paleolithic genius to leave the cookfire
and sketch with pity the panic in a hunted bison's eye.

3. *Speleology*

Tourists and experts have no place in caves.
We who dwell here lifelong are, as Plato feared,
indifferent both to splendor and to sanctuary. Driven
instead by rituals for invoking what we sense
hovers in the air to feed us, waits buried in the rock
for us to draw upon, we live obsessed by playing
with the light we've learned we can give off before we die.

PART IV

DEFINITIONS

Birth is the wound,
life the infection,
love the fever,
truth the chill,
memory the scab,
age the scar,
art the X ray,
death the cure.

POÈME NOIR

(a light-verse sonnet for audiences at readings)

Don't sweat it, baby. No need to stroke my hair,
peer, cluck, and murmur *Are you alright?*
because these new works growl, spit, roar
no signature chords of affirmation bright
as expectations. Despair had stature once
and poetry, not Prozac, cured. When I was touring
hell, I couldn't file dispatches since
hell was silence. Now that I can sing
again, hell is subject matter. As for the lover
who sent me there, well, tragic bards
are versed in writing wrongs past spite—an oeuvre
quite comic in this age of Hallmark Cards.
Such madness can be bittersweet brain candy.
So don't you sweat it, baby. I feel dandy.

COUNT DOWN

Survival is the final offer
that arrives at the eleventh hour
just when pain to the tenth power
would kill you with another ninth degree.

By then, relief strikes you brief as an eighth note;
you wear doom proudly; it's your seventh seal.
But life whispers through your sixth sense
of what might await you in some fifth dimension

where miracle is saved for the fourth quarter.
Tricked, you sigh and rise on the third day.
You know better, but with no second thought,
risk that first step—absurd as first love at first sight—

as if you were back at ground zero, as if it cost
nothing, as if this were not the last laugh.

TREE SISTER

For KM

Nothing lives that is not love at first—
if not sight, then understanding. All else is choice
of timing, no desire ever lost
completely, even if misplaced. Rejoice,
old friend—shy, wiry, naiad, bold
victim refusing as much pain as you dare—
your witchly laugh, your young face ageing
have not escaped me. You are a familiar lover
despite irrelevant facts. What do facts matter
when you and I have twined green fingers, branches,
limbs, leaves, blossoms, fruit together
across decades, in fantasies, through trenches?
Women still trying to learn what we know best:
how nothing lives that is not love at last.

BREAKTHROUGH BLEEDING

When memory, that phantom limb, has ceased to twinge;
when sweat fired in nightmare's oven hardens
to cool glaze; when dawn light stripes the floor
so sleep seems finally safe; when the heart rips raw
but free, trailing barbed wire behind it; when even
the rancid tongue at last rusts flakes of language,
forget forgiving.

A television documentary on seabirds, a gardening glove,
a photo that slipped to the back of a drawer—anything
will try to open the vein, unclot the hemhorrage. One day
with no warning the mantlepiece tilts free of its moorings,
crashes, spews old gifts of pottery all over the room.
Be grateful. Do not save the shards. Some breaks
can never be mended.

And should you ever find yourself barefoot again
at those familiar crossroads, broken glass paving the road
in every direction—choose any route. But dance along it this time,
laughing, because now you know the way. With practice,
you might be able to leave behind some sign of beauty
as you go, even if only a trail of dew glittering
red in the sun.

ACROBATS AND CLOWNS

You start out as the acrobat (everyone does)
sweating your balancing act
aglitter in sequined tights and resin,
muscles rigid with the strain of making it
look effortless, smiling down
at the upraised faces, bowing, wearing their roar
of approval under your satin cape warm
next to your skin.

You start out by defying death (everyone does),
but you long to be the best. So, with enough time,
skill, gall, practice, you raise hopes, standards,
price, expectations: you work without a net.
How they love you for it, how they throng
to hold their breath at what you risk in the gold light,
cheering, praying to claim your autograph
or be lucky enough to be there when you die.

Of course one day you fall—through the cracks,
out of favor, behind, short. Maybe some war in heaven
sends you tumbling head over heels on end for years
without a clue as to who was offended by your existence.
Maybe you fall in love, when the ringmaster invites

your soul to sing with a funky lowdown sound
so velvety you dance out on thin air. Maybe you fall for it,
for the lover swearing *you can trust me,* whispering *leap.*

Or maybe you just get tired and fall apart.
At least a thousand reasons, as many as the fragments
of you lying shattered on the sawdust.
They give you up for dead and piece you back together.
You're never quite the same.
But circuses are all you know, and you discover
a talent for being clumsy: simple, since all postures hurt,
and falling has become your way of life.

Whatever gods found you amusing before the fall
no longer interfere. Whatever lover you arched toward
now finds you merely entertaining. So you trade in
the spangled doublet and gilt crown
for an electric, bulbous nose, torn baggy pants,
trick suspenders, pompom buttons. Your hair,
grown wild as your gaze, is what works
without a net now, defying gravity.

Crowds bend their downturned heads to where you sprawl,
and smile. So you raise standards, hopes, and expectations,
exaggerate your blunderous art, start to forget
things, drop things, cower in terror.
The lions, perched on children's wooden stools, yawn.
But the crowd adores it, as you get chased, caught, tripped,

banged, set on fire, drenched, shot from a canon, run over,
squeezed into a barrel, screamed at for your pains.

You have stumbled on their secret: they fear grace
is a limited resource; the less you have the more is left
for them. That's why they love you now. But you notice
it's the babies who stare at you in awe, the grandparents
who weep, those in between who do the laughing.
Then, before you know it, the beam of light that's hunted you
down shrinks where you stand to a close and closing circle, inside
which, effortlessly, you dim, bow, smile, and fall at last asleep.

CHORDS

For Blake Morgan

Poised at this last, late lifetime's threshold, all my keys
in hand, I hear my young musician neighbor
through his door, wrestling his rhythms and melodies
across precision's crucible, over and over—

and think: we breathed the same air once. Now you compose
yourself despite each day's percussive toll;
know how to live for the play of making (and when to revise).
I smile. My dear, we breathe the same air still.

What secrets you'll need, you know: how to risk your life
but save your art; how to laugh bitterly, but love.
Our paths are different; mine narrows now; neither is safe.
It takes a poem to say that I can leave

behind alive in who you are the sole, sweet basic
before which words do gladly fail me. The rest is music.

CREATION MYTH

Each frame becomes part of the picture, requiring a larger
frame. I'd commuted the world for love—a sentence
harsh as the verdict that we are all only guests
in each other's lives—but knew enough to approach
the Dead Sea and Himalayas, lowest and highest

realms on earth, alone. One friend claims
in this age of jet travel it takes a while for the soul
to catch up with the body's arrival. Still, what survives
such flight returns distilled to its essence, alive
not in anyone's image, but deeply at furious peace.

Sightseers assume the great boulders in Central Park
are clever landscaping. Free now to sprawl in the sun
across them, I know they are over four hundred million
years old, ribs from the spine of crystalline bedrock
running under the surface of Manhattan Island.

Warm to my touch, these rocks are survivors of five
glacial ice sheets, the essence eroded from mountains
grand, once, as the Himalayas. Each edge
becomes part of the middle, requiring a further edge.
Today I walk the Great Road, as it was called

once—now Greenwich Avenue, then the vast highway
cleared by the Iroquois, stretching north into Canada
—and chant my songs with the other ghostly runners
who shimmer through leafgreen-dappled time. Each center
becomes part of the rim, requiring a deeper core.

Let there be words for the naming of just such a moment,
when I round the corner into this quiet street
where small calley pear trees exclaim their bloom sudden
as a white spring mist overarching the path to my building:
And the evening and the morning are the first day.